100 Quotes

"Life is worth living"

Emmanuel Aluko

DEDICATION

To all hardworking Parents

Disclaimer

Some of the quotes are not original work and may be similar to quotes attributed to other people. No claim is being made as the attribution of any of any of the 100 quotes to the author. The 100 quotes form an interesting collection of quotes which is hoped will inform people's lives

CONTENTS

Acknowledgments   i

The 100 quotes   1

About the author   24

ACKNOWLEDGMENTS

To my family, Roz, Elsie, Manuella and Jesse who give
me the motivation to keep going.

THE 100 QUOTES

1. Failing to plan is planning to fail.

2. The finding of absence is not the absence of finding.

3. Love what you do and do what you love.

4. You never have enough time to do something.

5. One can never be ready to embark on an adventure.

6. Timeliness is next to godliness.

7. The biggest risk you can take is not taking any risk.

8. Show me someone who has not failed, and I know they have not tried.

9. Be thoughtful with your words. Once said, it can never be retracted.

10. If at first you don't succeed, keep trying.

11. The only constant in life is change.

12. In the long run, we are all dead.

13. No amount of money is enough to sell your reputation.

14. This is a bank. Only money matters.

15.   A fool and her money are soon parted.

16.   Make your own luck by being lucky at making things.

17.   Success is mainly perspiration stained with inspiration.

18.   Practice, practice and keep practicing to achieve perfection.

19.   Success follows the hardworking, failure the hardly working.

20. There is no need to change a winning formula.

21. Innovate to survive, or stagnate to die.

22. Man has continuously achieved the impossible.

23. A lack of evolution may need to be corrected by revolution.

24. There may be a need for destruction prior to construction.

25.   It is better to be late than to never achieve a goal.

26.   A good sales pitch can sell, but only a good product can sustain selling.

27.   It is great to receive, but greater to give.

28.   If your country shows you love, you will love your country in return.

29.   A leader must be able to manage, but a

manager need not be a
leader.

30.   You can have
enough of what you
need, but never enough
of what you want.

31.   Be content with
what you have, and
what you don't have.

32.   The wise learn from
their mistakes, the
foolish make mistakes
for others to learn.

33.   One of the biggest
obstacles to achieving is

not believing it can be done.

34.   A reputation that has taken many years to build can be destroyed in no time.

35.   The prediction of experts should be treated with caution.

36.   Life is a marathon. Start slow, stay competitive in the middle and finish strongly.

37. Make life fair for you by doing the right things.

38. Do things right and do the right things always.

39. Do not stop educating yourself as knowledge is liberating.

40. Great gain normally comes with great pain.

41. The love of money undermines a person's character.

42. Doing things in a hurry can cost you more time.

43. The key to success is preparation.

44. Success has many friends, but failure is lonely.

45. Everyone needs a friend.

46. Treat people with respect, if you want respect from people.

47. Play hard, only after working hard.

48.   Better to work smart than to work hard.

49.   A job is for a period, while an occupation is for life.

50.   Patience is a virtue, but inertia is a sin.

51.   To enjoy success, one must endure failure.

52.   Working hard is hard work with rewards.

53.   Be a good listener, so your spoken words may be appropriate.

54. A checklist prevents you from forgetting what needs to be done.

55. Prioritize activities in terms of what is urgent and what is important.

56. Defer to your intuition, supporting it with data and knowledge.

57. Money does not buy happiness, but a lack of money can compromise happiness.

58. One lie is never enough to cover your tracks.

59. When you hear something many times, you start to believe it even if false.

60. Some people are never satisfied. The more they have, the more they want.

61. Remember you are infallible when you criticize someone's mistakes.

62.   A sound knowledge of statistics prevents you from being deceived.

63.   Don't buy something because it is cheap, but because you need it.

64.   You may need to repeat things a few times before people get the point.

65.   Fear and greed are the biggest emotions that affect business success.

66.   Sometimes, failure is not an option.

67.   Be careful of deals. They are sometimes a trap.

68.   If it is too good to be true, it's probably a lie.

69.   Do not procrastinate; do it now!

70.   Be careful of the smooth talking salesman as he is probably selling a dud.

71.   Take care of yourself, as your health is invaluable.

72.   It is better to lose fairly than to win unfairly.

73.   Communication is key to any successful relationship.

74.   Always ask for a better deal, as the worst that can happen is your current deal.

75.   Imitate those who have been successful. It works and bears less risk.

76. Watch what you write, as it stays forever.

77. Experiment in life, as you never know what you will get.

78. Manage your boss, just as your boss manages you.

79. Listen, read and do, so that your knowledge is active.

80. Wisdom is knowing when to speak and when to listen.

81.   Be careful about gifts you accept, as they may require you to do something against your conscience in the future.

82.   Coincidences do happen, so do not rush to conclude causation.

83.   Multiple coincidences are no coincidence at all.

84.   Do not keep someone in the same job forever, so that their work may be checked.

85. Your employees are number one. Treat them well and they will serve the customers like kings.

86. Conserve cash, as it will save you in a crisis.

87. Balance your emotions. Don't get too elated, neither too miserable.

88. It can be sometimes difficult to tell the difference between the truth and a lie.

89. Do not take an action when angry. You may live to regret it.

90. Poverty is a disease that is difficult to cure.

91. Being rich is relative to those around you.

92. To be a successful investor, you need to diversify, be diligent, be disciplined and be daring.

93. Differentiate between what you are willing to do and what you are able to do.

94.   There is good debt and there is bad debt. The good debt is the debt you do not need.

95.   A bank is most willing to help you when you least need help.

96.   Money, sex and drugs. Three things that undermine the powerful.

97.   The madness of markets is understood by no one.

98. Chance plays a part in life. Hope and pray you get one.

99. The true test of any relationship is when things go wrong.

100. What is your life's purpose? Answer this question, and you know why you are here.

ABOUT THE AUTHOR

The author is an educator and business person who has put these quotes together as a tool for personal and professional reflection. It is informed by the author's experiences as a parent, student, teacher, business person and Christian.